D1143176

An
Assemblage
of
19th Century
Horses & Carriages

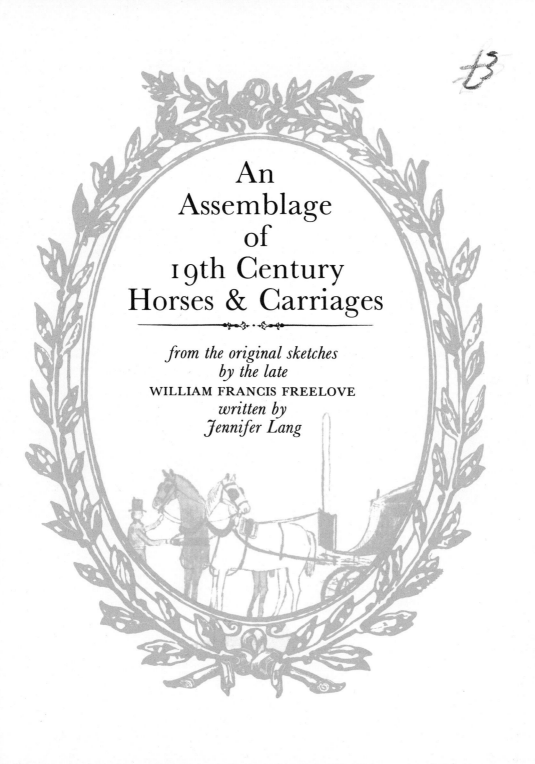

An Assemblage of 19th Century Horses & Carriages

from the original sketches
by the late
WILLIAM FRANCIS FREELOVE
written by
Jennifer Lang

First Edition published October 1971
by
Perpetua Press Downing Street Farnham Surrey

SBN 903070 00 6

Filmset by Photoset, London
Colour Separations by Photoset Reprographic, London
Printed by T. J. Press, London on a special making of
Conqueror Vellum Laid manufactured at
Wiggins Teape's Dover Mill.
Designed by Robin Ellis.
Bound in Buckram by Robert Hartnoll, Bodmin.

Up hill urge me not,
Down hill hurry me not,
Along the level spare me not,
And in the stable forget me not.

FROM AN ORNAMENTAL WINDOW IN A HANSOM CAB

Acknowledgements

The publisher would like to thank the many libraries, museums, institutions and private individuals who have provided help and encouragement throughout the production of *Horses & Carriages*, especially Miss Anne Bolt, Mr. A. Harris, Mr. H. Holmes, The Kingston upon Thames Public Library and Museum, Holborn Central Library, Mr. K. G. Rogers, The Society of Friends, The Science Museum, South Kensington and Mrs. F. C. Freelove, widow of Ernest Martin Freelove.

Introduction

WILLIAM FRANCIS FREELOVE
(1846-1920)

In 1871 a quiet young Quaker married a cooper's daughter from Kent and brought her home to Kingston. Queen Victoria had been on the throne for 33 years and the roads macadamized for even longer. With railways running the length and breadth of the country, communications had never been better, but William Freelove's contemporaries were still utterly dependent on the horsedrawn vehicle for the delivery of all things to all men. Although he probably never even rode a horse, let alone drove in a carriage, the young man was fascinated by the vehicles he saw around him. He was as interested in the slow plodding goods carts, as in the swift and gleaming private carriages.

Little is known about William Francis Freelove, except that he was a solicitors' clerk, he wrote well and was a good calligrapher. Like all good Victorian parents he and his wife, Elizabeth, had a large family—two sons and four daughters. Keeping a wife and bringing up a family of six, on a clerk's salary at the turn of the century required the strictest economy and there would have been no money to spare for toys for the children or expensive hobbies for their parents.

So to amuse his children and himself he began sketching these horses and carriages as he saw them in the streets around him. By 1873 he had produced a book of over 70 coloured sketches of every variety of business and pleasure vehicle to be seen in the vicinity of London. Entitled simply Horses & Carriages, it was not intended as a technical book or standard work. He painted for his own enjoyment and, beginning with the many ordinary vehicles, became more absorbed by his subject as he sought more bizarre equipages to add to his collection. The book was never published. Before he died he gave it to his youngest son, Ernest Freelove, and many year's later Ernest's widow passed it on to her nephew for his children. It was eventually discovered in an attic, among the usual sort of family jumble, and recognised as a fascinating commentary on the life-style and everyday scenes of nineteenth-century life.

Publishers Note

The sketches contained in the pages to follow are largely reproduced as they were found. We feel it worthy of explanation to mention that, where for instance the order of carriages and carts may to some seem strange, it has been the intention of the publisher not to alter the original format except where absolutely necessary for style or legibility. The paper on which the book is printed has been specially made to closely match the paper on which the originals were drawn a hundred years ago—consequently this book is not so much a technical or precise account of horsedrawn vehicles as a genuine book of entertainment although we know that to the enthusiast, collector and social historian the sketches will provide an unsurpassed account of Victorian life and transport.

INDEX

*This book is respectfully dedicated
to the memory of the late
William Francis Freelove*

Horses & Carriages

KINGSTON-UPON-THAMES OCT., 1873

Foreword

A hundred years in a nation's history is nothing, yet in terms of social change it can seem a long time. Scientific discoveries can accelerate a nation's development to such an extent that previously cherished possessions become obsolete almost overnight. One of these is the horse and carriage, which with the invention of the internal combustion engine, now has little place in the latter half of the twentieth century. Of course every generation is still influenced by the past. They copy their forefathers' furniture and serve preservation orders on their buildings. We admire Adam fireplaces, Nash Terraces and Wren churches. But however much we value the past we cannot recapture its tempo. We are carried inexorably along by the benefits of progress.

Ever since primitive man invented the wheel, he had been experimenting with horse-drawn vehicles, but it was not until Elizabeth I's reign that the first coach was introduced into England. From then on it was the object of the English designers' ingenuity and the coachbuilders' art. The development of the carriage was subject to many influences, including 'the king's business'. Diplomacy was carried out in person, or by despatches. Couriers had fast journeys to make across foreign countries, so that a coach had to serve as bedroom, sitting room and conveyance. The inside fittings were both elaborate and ingenious, yet the overall comfort achieved was limited by the inadequacies of the roads along which the coach had to travel. As long as it had to traverse the deep ruts, potholes and almost impassable bogs of the early roads, a coach had to be built to withstand these hazards and the horses had to be strong and heavy to pull its cumbersome weight. Only when Macadam's revolutionary approach to road surfaces improved English highways, did coaching become a reliable and fast mode of travel.

The period 1820-1840, known as the Golden Age of coaching, was the era after John Macadam's improvements and before the establishment of the railways. Many a song has been sung and scene painted of those glorious days. The plethora of galloping coaches and fours on every season's batch of Christmas cards, demonstrates how the aura of coaching still evokes nostalgic feelings in our jet-age.

There were several ways of travelling by coach—in the Royal Mail or stage coach, in a private travelling coach or hired postchaise. By the 1830's there were more than 700 Royal Mail coaches operating day and night and well over 3,000 stage coaches. The former, carrying the mail and a limited number of passengers, was king of the road.

All other traffic had to give way to it. Averaging sometimes more than 11 mph, and with an enviable reputation for punctuality, the Royal Mail operators always considered themselves far superior to the humbler stage. An opinion not shared by some of the stage coach companies, who took just as much pride in the service they provided and the appearance of their vehicles. The stage had room for more passengers and a great deal of luggage. All coachmen had to be skilled drivers and were assisted by the guard, who alerted toll keepers of their approach, with sonorous blasts on the 'yard of tin'. Guards of a musical bent indulged their talent to great effect. Beneath every coach of whatever kind, there hung a device shaped like a shoe, to be slipped beneath the hind wheel when descending steep hills, and it was one of the duties of the guard to perform this task on every descent where the gradient might have been too sharp for the wheelers to hold the coach unaided.

Travelling post—either in your own coach or a hired postchaise—was an expensive business, costing 1/6d a mile. It was accomplished by the aid of postboys. These small, light men, who drove the coach from the saddles of the near side horses were a tough and outspoken breed, from whom the name postillion is derived. Constantly in the saddle, galloping through all weathers, with the idiosyncracies of private owners to allow for, they developed their own brand of stubborn independence, which most travellers learnt to respect—since without a postboy your journey could not progress very far or fast. They were based at the numerous posting houses along the roads, as horses needed to be changed about every 15 miles to travel at any speed. These establishments varied tremendously in the standard of horses and hospitality they offered, but all of them were geared to accommodate the horses and refresh the travellers.

The best days of coaching were short lived, for not long after the improvement of the roads, came a new kind of improvement—the railways. The design of carriages was affected. From large, luggage carrying equipages needing successive teams of horses, the fashion changed to smaller carriages, which were more manoeuvrable. The horse and carriage was just as indispensable for shorter journeys not covered by the railways, and there was no slackening of work for the many different trades which relied on carriage business.

One of the most vital links in the chain of support was the business of job-master, similar to that of a car hire firm today. They were dedicated to supplying their clients with the best possible equipage—from the shine on the coachman's buttons down to the last lick of paint on the wheels. They ranged from the job-masters who had hundreds of horses in their stables and a high reputation for the quality of their horses, the gleam on their harness and the perfection of their carriages, to the little one-man business who was on hire to the casual trade. The big ones usually only did contract work. Many private people found jobbing a better alternative to owning their own coaches, and hired by the year from a job-master. Such contracts were the jam on his business; the bread and butter was the work he did for commercial firms.

An important aspect of the job-master's business was supplying horses. One London job-master, who had 400 horses working in carriage and commercial work in the city of London, also had over 2,000 horses out on permanent hire to people who had their own carriages and servants, but who preferred to leave the provision of horsepower to the expert. If a horse went sick or lame, they just notified the job-master and a replacement was brought round by the 'cob boy' immediately. So apart from being a stickler for spit and polish, the job-master had also to be a good judge of horseflesh. His hunting grounds were the fairs and shows around the country, where the dealers came with hundreds of strings of horses to tempt a wary buyer. The job-master would travel the countryside picking up 40 horses here and 50 there. Naturally, even a really wily trader could not always be sure that he didn't have one or two rogues in his string. There was often the problem, after schooling and breaking to carriage work, of what to do with an unsuitable horse; one who was either too slow, too unsteady, or just unsuitable for any job in the stable. The great repository for such unsatisfactory animals was the trams. Little was required of a horse who pulled a tram other than to keep going in a forward direction. No smooth action or honest temper was needed.

The best horses were the ones which came on regular boatloads from Holland. The far-sighted Dutchmen who had an eye for the good in the Cleveland Bays, bought up most of the mares and transported them from Yorkshire back to Holland. There they were crossed with a good Dutch stallion and the strain jealously guarded by exporting only the geldings to England. These big bay horses proved some of the best for carriage work. When they came to England as four-year-olds, they were already as quiet as lambs, having been worked on the Dutch farms since the age of two. They did 10 years of excellent carriage work, and when they were slowing up a little could be switched to drawing a commercial delivery van. By the time they were 18 and too old for hard work, there were still farmers prepared to buy them for the slower work on the farm; though of course the farmers were not keen on having a gelding, because they preferred a mare which might yield a foal a year in addition to her use on the farm.

The job-master is one of the last links with the carriage industry still remaining. One or two of the most adaptable are still in business. Their main work is supplying the television and film industries. Hardly a period play goes by that doesn't have a horse and carriage somewhere in the script. Among the customs and traditions of our modern society, there are still occasions when someone wants a coach and four—a wedding or a pageant which needs the pomp and circumstance of horses. For such occasions the job-master can still provide the solution.

Pleasure Vehicles

The nineteenth century was an age of expansion and consolidation. The merchant venturers had made fortunes overnight and rich men were eager to display their new found wealth. More and more, carriages became a symbol of status and prestige. The image-conscious publicity men of the twentieth century are but following the precepts of an earlier age, when one of the most important indications of a man's standing in the world was the outward appearance he created. His house, his servants and especially his carriages were all evidence of his affluence.

The grandest carriage in a nobleman's stable was his town coach or state carriage. This was fairly old fashioned in design, sumptuously painted in the family colours, with armorial bearings. It was so well built as to be almost indestructible, and was driven by a liveried coachman, with two or four footmen up behind, carrying gilded weighted staves, with which to repel footpads, thieves and robbers. Many such coaches still survive and one or two are in use today. The Town Coach in the Royal Mews is used on state occasions and by ambassadors presenting their credentials to the Crown.

But life was speeding up in the nineteenth century. It was not always convenient to get out all the paraphernalia of the state coach for a short journey into the city. In 1838 Lord Brougham—then Lord Chancellor of England—started a fashion for a smart closed carriage that could be pulled by only one horse. Named after its instigator, the brougham became the most popular simple town carriage for gentlemen until the end of the carriage era. It cost £100 to build and with only one horse needed to draw it, was comfortable, economic and manoeuvrable.

The brougham was the perfect gentleman's carriage when travelling alone, but for the ladies' and the family's everyday journeys the larger landau was necessary. This was an all-purpose carriage, which could be either closed or open. A landau carried four people and had a box for the coachman and carriage groom, who attended to the comfort of the passengers and of the horses. A footman would have been excellent in handing the ladies in and out of the carriage, but would have been little use to the coachman in the event of the horses being startled into some disastrous action. With the hoods up a landau was roomy, comfortable and snug on cold and wet days; yet on fine days the two hoods folded back and allowed the occupants to get the full benefit of the warm air.

It may seem strange to us, in this pollution-conscious age, that our predecessors drove out so regularly to enjoy the air. A drive round the park with no exhaust fumes to mar it was a pleasant afternoon's occupation. This custom produced a large variety of open four-wheeled carriages, designed to be owner-driven, called phaetons. The phaeton originated in the fast and furious Regency days, when men of rank first took up driving as a sport. Fashion was set by the court and the court favourites, and the Highflyer Phaeton, having first found favour with a trend-setting prince, soon appeared in numerous different disguises, such as the Mail, Stanhope, Park and Spider phaetons. By Victorian times the self-driven vehicle had become more respectable, and a lady was no longer in danger of losing her reputation if she went dashing about the country in a young man's new phaeton and pair.

The Park Phaeton was considered ideal for ladies venturing into the park for their daily drive. The body was specially shaped to display their voluminous crinolines to advantage and the little seat at the back was just big enough to take the diminutive groom called a 'tiger'. This carriage was light enough to be drawn by a pair of perfectly mannered ponies. A high standard of schooling and behaviour was expected of these ponies, as the fair lady driver, though often expert, was not expected to have any strength of arm to hold a strong-headed pair. Her parasol whip was for decoration only and floated above her head like a flag. The ponies were spirited enough to spank through the park at high speed, but when she saw a friend with whom she wanted to exchange whispered confidences, they were expected to stand quietly without fidgeting.

In these days of mass production, anything built specially to your own design seems the height of luxury. In Victorian days all carriages were made specifically for the owner. So although they fell broadly into categories they all varied in detail, according to the owner's taste. The "Carriage seen in Bushey Park" is an example of how far variations could go. The owner of this carriage seems to have been a man of such imagination that his contemporaries failed completely to classify his carriage. Half-way between a landau and a brougham, it is something of a hybrid. The driver is obviously not a professional coachman—since he is not in livery, nor is he holding his whip. All good coachmen carried their whips when they were driving. The apparel he is sporting seems to be more the uniform of the turf; the jolly duo in the dickie seat on the back are liberally rewarding the urchins with coins for their cartwheels. It would seem that William Freelove caught a happy party on its way home from a successful day's racing.

The irrepressible children on London's streets often used to show complete disrespect for the dignity of the gentry, by using their smart carriages for free rides. Some broughams had rear spikes built in to prevent a mob of small ragamuffins hampering their progress.

Country life was an important part of Victorian England. With little to disturb the even tenor of the days, much time was spent in visiting neighbouring families. A useful carriage for this exercise was the capacious waggonette. It was very popular with Prince Albert—who in his time was almost as influential on the taste of the day as the Prince Regent had been in his. For families who employed a coachman, the waggonette was a good country vehicle—less formal than the landau. Costing about 50 gns., it was within the means of families of modest, though not straitened, circumstances. The seats could be removed to accommodate a quantity of baggage, and some people by adding a superstructure and solid roof converted it to a closed carriage. One enterprising job-master advertised himself as having carriages and horses available for every occasion, but in fact all he had was one waggonette and a pair of hard worked horses. Nevertheless, he did a roaring trade with this adaptable vehicle by judicious manipulation of the roof and seats.

A more utilitarian type of country carriage, was the dog-cart. Originally designed for carrying guns and dogs for shooting parties, it soon became a most useful conveyance for everything. It had a large box-like space, with slatted sides, for the dogs, and could be drawn by one horse, or occasionally two, driven tandem. Tandem driving was one of the most difficult of all since the leading horse, out in front on his own, had no second horse beside him to guide or settle him down, as in a team. The driver had to succeed in making the leader go on and the wheeler stay back in order to achieve a smart and effective balance between the two horses.

A dog-cart driven tandem was a convenient way of getting to the meet on hunting mornings. The leading horse had little work to do drawing the cart and was unharnessed upon arrival and saddled for the day's sport. The other horse and vehicle were left in the groom's charge, whose job it was to be on hand at the end of the day to reharness the second horse and drive the tired sportsman back home to his warm fireside.

The dog-cart soon began to appear at more than sporting events. The doctor used it for his rounds, the farmer for his visits to the fairs, the parson for his calls of mercy. There were a great many families in the country who had neither the wherewithal, nor the need, to run large stables and keep a great many carriages. They had no coachman only a sturdy cob, but with a dog-cart they could still travel around the countryside in comfort.

A number of carriages were designed with the more domestic needs of a large family in mind. Children learnt to drive at an early age, or were driven by female companions in a variety of small vehicles, built close to the ground and drawn by safe and steady ponies. The basket chaise was a typical example. With a wicker-work finish it had no paint to be scratched by flailing little feet and was light enough to be within the power of one small pony. The Moray—or village cart—was a simple vehicle on which a young learner driver could practise his skill. Small and semi-circular in shape, there was room for four people sitting back to back, with the driver facing the pony.

All of these vehicles here described accommodated only four people, with additional space being taken up by the coachman and groom. Considering the size of the average Victorian family, one wonders how on earth they all managed to get about. On occasions when the whole family wanted to go out together a brake would have carried them all. These large vehicles could be drawn by two or four horses. They can still occasionally be seen today, at shows and fairs, with a team of horses—giving rides to enthusiasts anxious to emulate, if only for a moment, the style of their predecessors.

Freelove has confused a body break with a four-in-hand drag, which is in fact the name given to an owner-driven coach. Ever since it became possible to get some speed out of the horsedrawn vehicle, there has always been a very sporting element in driving. The fashion for driving your own coach came into vogue when the railways took over from the stage and mail coaches as a means of transport. The famous Four-in-hand Club was formed in 1856 and some years later The Coaching Club. The latter is still flourishing today. On a lovely day in June 1871 the first meet of The Coaching Club was held in Hyde Park, when 21 coaches assembled at Marble Arch and drove to the Trafalgar at Greenwich, led by Lord Carrington. A hundred years later The Coaching Club celebrated its centenary when 14 owner-driven coaches attended a meet in Hampton Court Palace. Membership is exclusive and limited to those who have been seen competently driving a four-in-hand.

In 1873, by no means had all coaches disappeared from the scene. There were enough enthusiastic supporters of travel by coach for many companies to continue running coaches on well-tried and popular runs. The London to Brighton, Oxford to Cambridge and London to Southampton runs were still regularly running coaches. Kingston would have been a staging post on the London Guildford road and Freelove must have seen the Guildford coach many times changing horses on its way to and fro.

The poor man's coach was the pleasure van. It cost a penny a ride and was a good day's outing for high days and holidays. Many firm's used to hire them for an annual office spree for all their employees. Very often this was all the holiday a poor family would get.

But life for the wealthy was practically all holiday and would certainly have included a month by the sea for the family. Once there, one of the favourite pastimes for the children would be driving in the goat chaises—rather like donkey rides today. The goat chaise was a strong little carriage and apart from being the joy and delight of countless small infants at Ramsgate and Margate, it had a more practical application. For families who could not rise to the level of a horse or carriage, it was often the only form of conveyance. A pair of goats was all the livestock they needed—the nanny to provide them with milk and the billy to act as beast of burden.

1

——— STATE CARRIAGE ———

2

——— CHILDRENS GOAT CHAISE ———

BASKET CHAISE

PAIR OF PONIES
seen in Richmond Park

TANDEM DOG-CART

ONE HORSE BROUGHAM

— PAIR HORSE WAGGONETTE —

— PAIR HORSE HOODED PHAETON —

9

FOUR IN HAND DRAG

10

PLEASURE VAN

———— CARRIAGE ————
seen in Bushey Park   (name unknown)

———— VILLAGE CART ————

LANDAU *(open)*

LANDAU *(closed)*

THE ·· GUILDFORD ·· COACH

1813

LONDON TO GUILDFORD—30 MILES

Business Vehicles

William Freelove's interest in commercial vehicles makes his book a fascinating study of late nineteenth-century life. Plenty of famous artists spent their time drawing and painting the flamboyant coaches and grand carriages of their era. But few contemporary painters have been interested enough in humble carts to painstakingly record the everyday conveyances they saw on the street. The carriages of the rich were built to last, and finished with four or five coats of paint. Many were kept in dry coach houses, lavishly cared for by the coachman, and passed down through the family as heirlooms. Not so the humble costermonger's barrow. By the time it had finished a knock-about life, there was little to recommend it to posterity. It was worked hard until it fell to pieces, then used for firewood or sold as scrap.

Though more advanced than the Cries of London of Restoration times, the delivery methods of 100 years ago are a long way from our clinical packaging today. Freelove, on his way to his office in the mornings, watched the butcher, the baker and the candlestick-maker driving round from door to door. Milk was not left in a bottle on the doorstep. The milk-man drove by with his churn and ladled out the required amount straight into the housewive's milk jug. The horse waited patiently between the shafts while business was transacted. He made the trip each day and knew exactly when to move on to the next stop. At the end of the day he would turn for home and arrive at his stable without any guidance from his tired master. One tradesman remembers a little donkey, which pulled a costermonger's barrow, making nothing of drawing a ton of potatoes over Kew Bridge—provided the female 'jenny' had been left behind in the stable.

In the nineteenth century, people had to work hard. The worse thing that could happen to you was to lose your job, but almost as bad was to lose your means of livelihood. To many, the horse was the means. If it were sick the master could not go out to work. Physicking of animals therefore was a rough and ready business, mainly performed by the owners. There were violent cures, incorporating the use of gin and whisky, designed to keep the horse on the road at all costs.

A few carts which did survive were successfully converted to mechanised transport. In particular the tip carts, used for bricks, coal and heavy cargo, had a mechanism at the front to tip up and deposit their loads where required. Many a tractor on small farms in the north of England is now trundling round with an old converted tip cart as a trailer.

For one or two horsedrawn delivery vans there was still a need in the twentieth century, as a few firms still wished to reserve for their best customers an extra flourish in the art of delivery. The carriages of Lock's the hatters, and Fortnum and Mason, were a familiar sight in London's streets, until the 1970's. Gilbey's used to deliver champagne to Buckingham Palace in a coach and four. But the high cost of stabling and the scarcity of the right men to work with horses, have closed the stables of all but a few. Rothman's 100 year old delivery brougham still makes a daily journey to the Rothman showroom in St. James's Street; the Watney advertising brougham can regularly be seen taking yeast from the brewery to Watney House in Victoria.

Many firms now in the forefront of mechanised transport, first began trading with horses. One of the oldest of these is Pickford's, who have been in the removal business since the packhorse era. One Thomas Pickford was seized by the Roundheads in 1646 supposedly for supplying horses to the Cavaliers. The early Pickford carriers ran their business from Poynton in Cheshire which led to over a century and a half of horse and waggon trade between Manchester and London. They also made use of the canals for quick and efficient transport of goods and subsequently the railways. By Freelove's time, Pickford's were agents for the cartage of goods on the railways, as well as in business removing personal household effects by horsedrawn waggon.

It is the brewers who cling most tenaciously to the traditions of the horsedrawn vehicle. The connection goes back to the posting days, when the comfortable progress of every journey depended upon the hospitality of the post establishments on the route. Many of these are now public houses with a strong coaching tradition. Out of a total of just under a hundred brewery companies, some dozen still use horses for deliveries. This may sound archaic today, but withstands the test of economic sense. When the time and motion men arrived at Young's brewery in Wandsworth, they encountered the horses there with shocked incredulity, only to find, when they went into the cost effectiveness, it was not so antiquarian as it seemed, and Youngs have kept their horses for delivery of beer within a 3 mile radius. Adnams have just reverted to using horses again, as a more efficient means of transporting beer from the brewery to their pubs.

Waggons today are drawn by a pair of shire horses, or sometimes a 'unicorn' is used— a third horse in front of the two wheelers, as in Freelove's picture of the Romford Brewery Van. In the last century practically every town of reasonable size had its own brewery, and Romford was no exception. In 1791 the Star Inn Brewery was founded there. A Mr. Ind and a Mr. Mashiter then started a brewing firm in the 1830's. Mr. Mashiter was replaced by a Mr. Coope and the firm of Ind Coope & Co. swallowed up the Star Inn and renamed it the Romford Brewery Co. Ind Coope has now in turn been overtaken and is part of Allied Breweries.

Although some breweries still retain horses for daily work, the original vehicles themselves are not so practicable. Whitbread's have in their stables a fine example of an old Brewers Dray and also an original Brewery Van, but the actual deliveries are made in four-wheeled waggons, almost identical to a Pickford's furniture van of the 1870's. In addition to their working routine Whitbread grey shire horses play their part in ceremonial up and down the land, including an annual appearance drawing the Lord Mayor's Coach from the Mansion House to the Law Courts.

For breweries with horses, showing is an integral part of the stable routine. The head coachman at Young's is away as much as six months a year competing. The biggest percentage of team and turn-out entries are from breweries. Young's, Watney Mann, Courage, Vaux and Thwaites are all regular prize-winners with pairs and teams of heavy horses. The Royal Lancs show, although smaller than those at Peterborough, Yorkshire and Kenilworth, has the greatest concentration, as it is in the heart of the heavy horse country.

Shows and fairs were excellent market places a hundred years ago for the horse-dealers. Success in the show ring could not but increase a seller's appeal to potential customers. Among coachbuilders, competition was hot, and a prize-winning design at the Royal Show was enough to tip the scales in your favour. Coachbuilders' catalogues advertised their wares as "Royal Society's First Prize Pair-horse waggon" and "Royal Society's Harvest Cart". Among those still showing today, there is high respect for the standards of the past. To so much as qualify for the Royal Show, let alone win a prize, you had to achieve the most exacting standards of perfection.

The shire horse we see in the show-ring today is a finer boned breed—after being crossed with the Scottish Clydesdale earlier this century—than the heavier horses of the past. For the work he was required to do, the old shire horse had to have strength and stamina before looks. Even then, a great number of horses could be needed to move a heavy load. One senior coachman still remembers having seen as many as fourteen horses harnessed one in front of the other to pull a gigantic piece of timber. Indeed today there are inaccessible places where only horses can go, and the Forestry Commission still use shire horses for moving timber, when a mechanical vehicle is unsuitable.

Some waggons could manage well enough with a good, strong shire horse until they came to a steep hill. Here there would be what was called a 'chain horse' waiting at the bottom, which would be fastened in front of the horse and waggon to produce the extra horsepower to reach the top. These horses cost a penny a time—and some wily drivers would dispense with their assistance if their own horse was at all capable of struggling up on its own. But he would not forget to charge his boss the penny for the chain horse. Thus a journey repeated six times rendered sixpence for the driver's own pocket, which in 1873 was a welcome supplement to a man's daily wage.

Among these sketches there are some delightful illustrations of how livestock was transported. Calves, sheep, pigs, and even cattle, were all dependent on the faithful horse for transport. The only thing you never saw in those days was a horse-box. Apart from the railways, which were expensive, the best way of transporting a horse was to harness it to a cart. The tigers' cage in Edmonds Menagerie would not have needed a team of six horses to draw it. But the circus, of which they were a part, used horses in other acts, who were harnessed to the waggons when the show was on the move. The only cart needed for the horse was the dead horse cart—a two-wheeled knacker's cart fitted with a winch on the back for winding on the corpse.

In any big commercial firm much schooling and breaking of horses was necessary. For this exercise a young horse, paired with an older and steadier companion, would be harnessed to a skeleton break—a mere shell of a vehicle designed to withstand all sorts of catastrophe. It had a high box at the front for the driver, well out of range of dangerous hind quarters, behind which was a tiny platform where a groom rode, ready to jump off and soothe the horses if the behaviour of the young one threatened them with imminent disaster. Breaking-in shire horses was a different technique with a different objective. They were schooled in their traces, with the coachman walking on foot behind. Only when they had learnt to progress sedately and stop at a word of command, were they harnessed to any vehicle. For once a team of powerful shire horses gets going with a heavy load, no man can stop them. He must assert his mastery with a word, as he has no hope of controlling them by force.

In our enthusiasm for the horse and carriage, it is easy to think that all our modern traffic problems are the inevitable consequence of the internal combustion engine. But of course distance lends enchantment. Large cities, had frequent chaotic traffic jams and in narrow streets the stench from horsedung was as bad as that from diesel fumes today, though not perhaps as harmful to the lungs. When only private carriages and commercial delivery vans were competing for space the situation was bad, but with the appearance in the 1820's of the omnibuses, and the increase in Hackneys for hire, conditions became as bad as ours today. In 1878, 237 people were killed and 3,961 injured in the streets of London.

The introduction of the omnibus brought travel within the reach of the ordinary middle class citizen, although early buses were not very enticing to the timid or faint-hearted traveller. The first to appear in 1829, were too large for London's narrow streets and were soon replaced by smaller vehicles carrying only 12 passengers inside and a few more on top. The demand for public transport brought many operators into the field, but the competition between rival bus companies and the disreputable character of their drivers, brought much notoriety and frightened away some potential customers.

By the end of the nineteenth century, however, the London General Omnibus Company had established a respectable and reliable service. Founded in 1856, it continued until the end of the horsedrawn era. Each vehicle had a capacity of 28 persons, and at the turn of the century there were still 2,000 horses in its stables.

The alternative to the omnibus was the tram. With its own brakes and rails on which to run, little was required from the horses, except power. Consequently the dud horses ended up on the trams, where they could do little damage. Old-fashioned horsedrawn trams are still operating in Douglas, Isle of Man, from the first week in May until the last week in September. The horses alternate in two hour shifts— providing pleasure to the tourist and profit—to the tune of £7,000 p.a.—to the council.

Finally, no city's transport would be complete without 'cabs'. Carriages for hire appeared in England in 1605—not long after the appearance of the first coach. But they were cast-off noblemen's coaches, which had seen better days, and were cold, uncomfortable and smelly. The first hackneys to be built especially for hire were the two-wheeled cabriolets, which appeared in 1823. Hence the nickname 'cab'. They were supplanted later by the four-wheeled hackney and the two-wheeled Hansom cab, both of which continued in competition with each other until the end of the carriage era. The former—nicknamed 'growler' because of the noise its four wheels made on the cobbled streets—could carry four people and a quantity of luggage on the roof. Its more dashing rival sacrificed space to speed and only accommodated two people and no luggage. Patented by John Hansom in 1834, it did not become fashionable until modified by John Chapman two years later. It was driven from a small seat at the back, and had a trap-door in the roof through which the passengers could speak to the driver. Hansom cabs were smart and rakish carriages. A lady endangered her reputation if she travelled in one unaccompanied. Some of the drivers were sons of ruined noblemen or impoverished squires, who took great pride in the appearance presented by themselves and their vehicles. Driving a high-stepper and with a jaunty bow tied to his whip, many such a gentleman by diligent pursuit of custom, earned £2-£3 a day. In the evenings he could return to the pursuits more expected of his birth and breeding and might even find himself consorting with some of the passengers who provided him with his income.

Hansom cabs of Freelove's time had absurdly small side windows, which were later replaced by bold plate-glass windows furnished with blinds for the benefit of the occupants' privacy. The earlier window was often a dummy—an object of art and adornment. Many a Hansom cab owner relieved his longings for armorial bearings by the intricate decoration or neat composition on his ornamental window. Indeed the one found by Freelove on a Hansom cab of his day bears a poem which is the quintessence of a good driver's respect for his horse.

——— COAL WAGGON ———

——— COSTERMONGERS BARROW ———

——— BUTCHERS CART ———

——— BAKERS CART ———

20

FISHMONGERS CART

21

MILK CART

22

———— WATER CART ————

23

———— HAY CART ————

PIANO CART

TALLOW CHANDLERS CART

————— ICE MERCHANTS CART —————

————— MILLERS or CORN DEALERS CART —————

STONE & MARBLE CART

FAT CATTLE CART

30

——— DEAD HORSE CART ———

31

——— BREWERS DRAY———

TIMBER CARRIAGE

BREAK

——— THREE HORSE OMNIBUS ———

——— TRAMWAY CAR ———

——— FOUR WHEELED CAB ———

——— HANSOM CAB ———

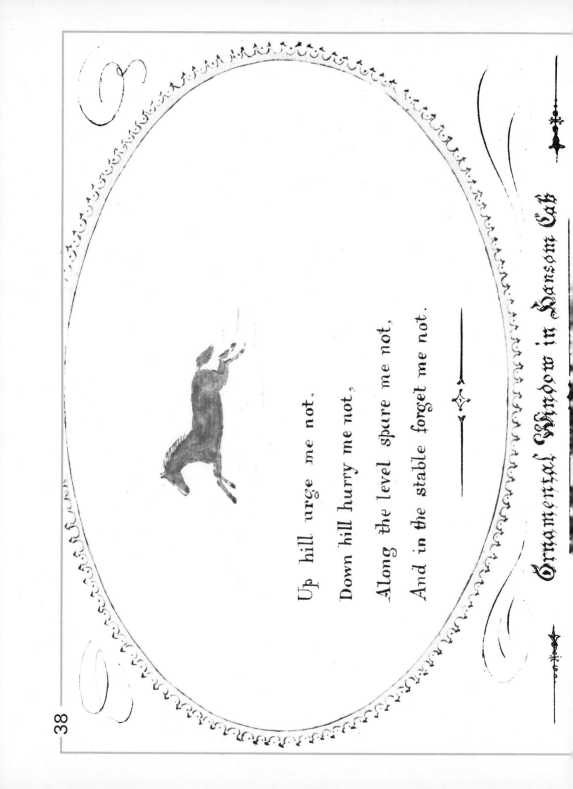

Up hill urge me not,

Down hill hurry me not,

Along the level spare me not,

And in the stable forget me not.

Ornamental Window in Hansom Cab

38

CHEAP JACKS VAN

CALF CART

CALF, SHEEP & PIG VAN

——— ROMFORD BREWERY VAN ———

——— SKIN CART ———

44

RAILWAY CART

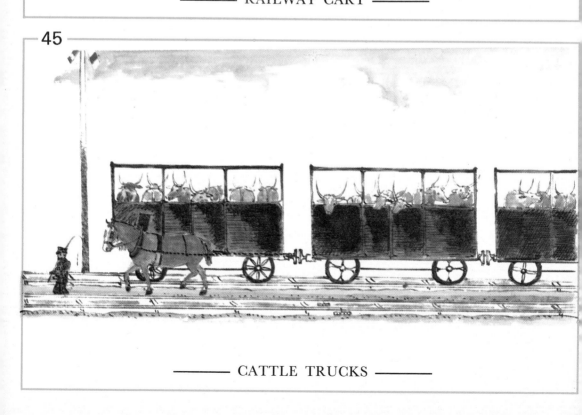

45

CATTLE TRUCKS

—— MILLERS WAGGON ——

—— TIMBER CARRIAGE ——

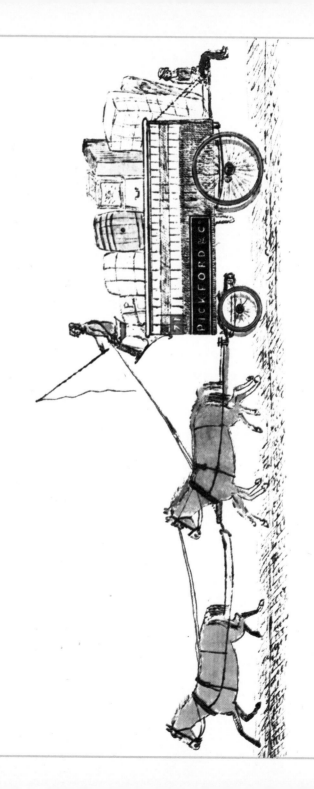

THREE HORSE VAN

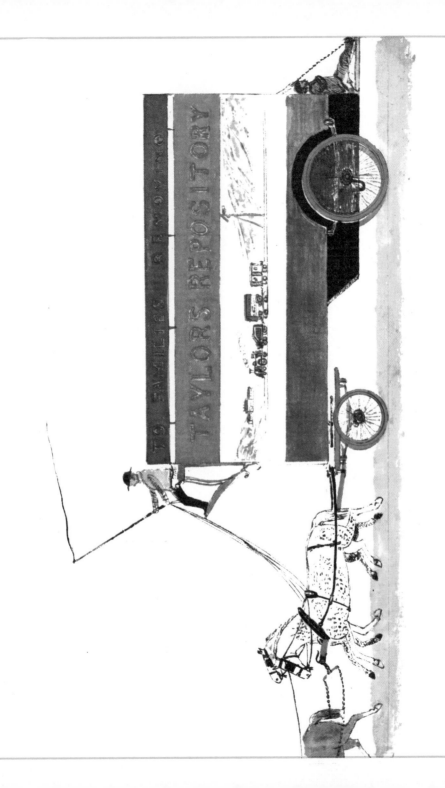

FURNITURE VAN

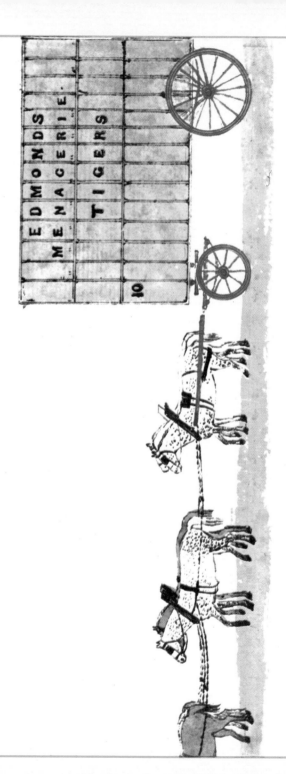

TRAVELLING MENAGERIE

BRICK CARTS

52

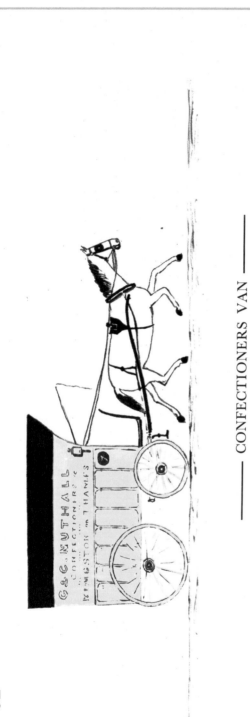

——— CONFECTIONERS VAN ———

53

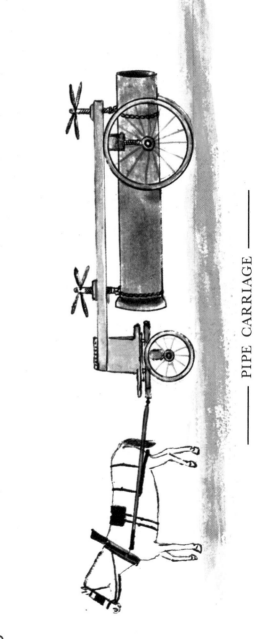

——— PIPE CARRIAGE ———

BOAT CARRIAGE

CARRIERS CART

(*in Winter*)

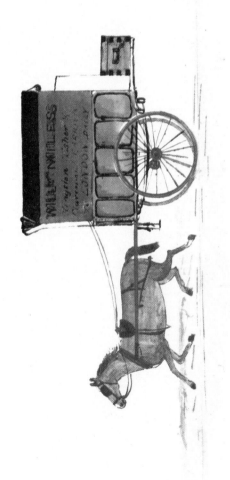

CARRIERS CART

(in Summer)

PLATE GLASS VAN

GLASS BOTTLE VAN

COAL MINE

ROAD SCRAPER & MUD CART

———— MILLINERY VAN ————

———— CASK CART ————

Special Vehicles

A horse is to ceremonial what the fairy is to pantomime, and for special effects there is nothing like a carriage and four. In Great Britain we are lucky still to have a Monarchy and all the horsedrawn paraphernalia which surrounds it. There are still 44 carriage horses in the Royal Mews and some 33 equipages. Britain is the only country which still provides carriages for diplomatic representatives, presenting their credentials to the Crown. Queen Alexandra's State Coach, The Glass Coach, The Town Coach and the landaus have all carried Ambassadors, and are driven by a coachman from the box. High Commissioners ride in Semi-State landaus, which are postillion driven. The broughams and landaus are a familiar sight in London and once or twice a year, for the opening of Parliament or a State visit, the pageant loving crowds are rewarded by the glittering spectacle of the full panoply of State in all its horsedrawn splendour.

Apart from royal occasions, carriages are still in demand from people wanting to cut a dash at special functions. A bride and groom seeking an original theme for their wedding, hire a coach and four or a carriage and pair. Of course in 1873 there was nothing original about arriving at a wedding in a carriage. Yet the display-conscious Victorians managed to make it into an occasion. A stream of landaus with four horses postillion ridden bringing guests to the church was not seen everyday. The horses wore white ear coverings and white tassels, and the postillion riders had white bows attached to their whips.

For solemn ceremonial a good Victorian funeral was unmatched. No motorised cavalcade can equal the solemnity of a procession of carriages at walking pace—every horse a black one and covered with black crepe. The funeral bier itself was drawn by six horses, and the more carriages attending him to the grave in solemnity, the more successful in life a man was presumed to have been. To attain the required pitch of stygian gloom all the horses and carriages, with their full complement of mutes and mourners, had to be hired from the undertaker. Such a burial was an expensive gesture of respect, costing between £60 and £100 for an upper tradesman to £1,000-£1,500 for a nobleman. The Irish are the great exponents in the art of a funeral. At many good Irish wakes today horses in black still draw the hearse and the relatives attend in mourning coaches.

Some of the last horsedrawn vehicles to disappear were the mail vans, which were operated by private individuals on contract to the Post Office. There were still 200 horsedrawn vans in London in May 1930, plodding noisily to and from the various railway termini, delivering letters, newspapers and parcels. They surprisingly carried no lamps before 1889. Although it was not to be supposed that they were responsible for all the injured pedestrians knocked down in London, they were the object of a considerable campaign launched by the Society for Prevention of Street Accidents and Dangerous Driving. This tenacious body, after 18 years of endeavour, finally persuaded the Postmaster General of the day to express a wish that all mail vans should carry lamps after dark.

The Metropolitan police did not own their own vehicles until 1858—prior to that they hired them, using a civilian driver. But by 1873 the horsedrawn Black Maria would have been a common sight, complete with a guard on the back carrying a naval 'hangar' with which to ward off any attack. If the prisoner were thought to be dangerous a mounted police escort accompanied the van, the police officers had very clear instructions not to enter into any conversation with the prisoner. The horsedrawn Black Maria was used by the Metropolitan police until 1922.

One of the most colourful vehicles on the streets was the fire engine. The efficient quenching of a fire depended on the quick appearance on the scene of two vehicles— the steam fire engine and the fire tender, which carried the fire brigade. When the alarm was sounded the boiler on the steam engine would be lit as the horses were being put to, and while the contraption was galloping to the stricken building, the fire in the boiler would be gathering momentum. By the time the second vehicle arrived, with the dozen or so firemen, the steam would be reaching maximum pressure in the boiler and was ready to activate the pump to get the water supply to the flames.

WEDDING CARRIAGES

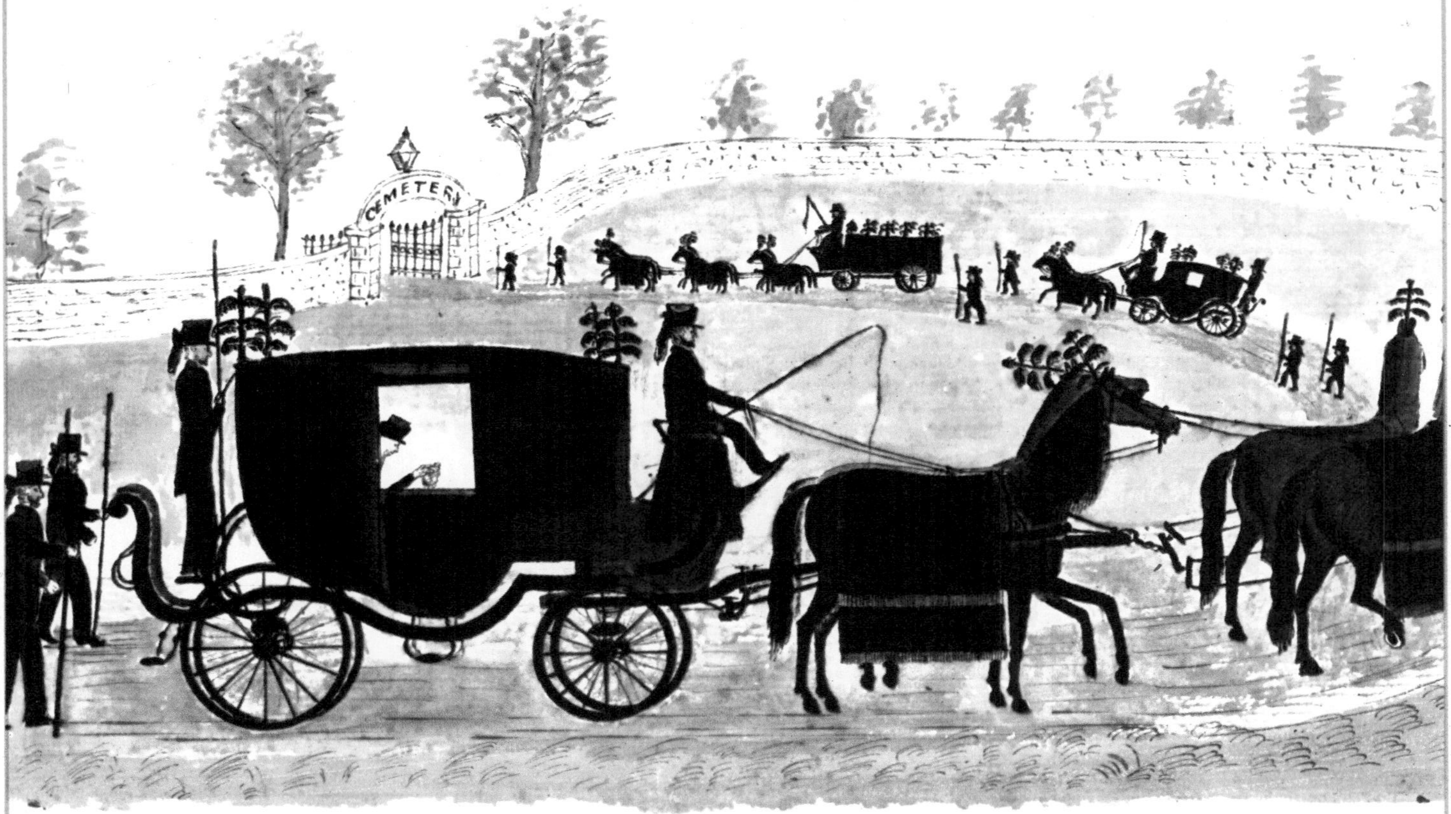

HEARSE & MOURNING COACHES

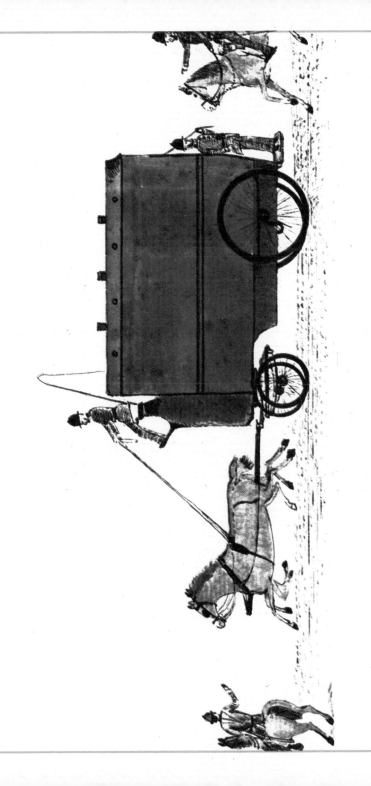

POLICE or PRISON VAN

FIRE ENGINE

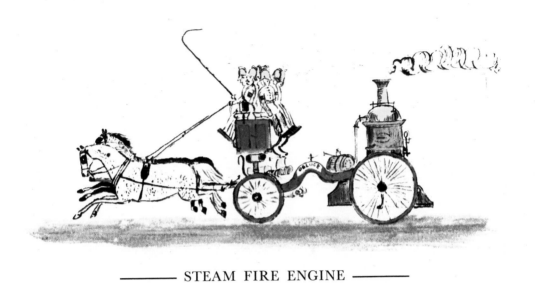

STEAM FIRE ENGINE

Nondescript

When a horse was old and tired and unfit for work, all that stood between him and a bullet from the knacker's yard was the bathing machine proprietor. Years of pounding the cobbled streets in a commercial van, would have given such a droop to his shoulders, sores to his body and trouble in his legs that he would only be of use on a beach, where business was booming, due to the popularity of the new sport of bathing.

The bathing machines lined the water's edge and the modest bather was able to equip himself for the sea, discreetly hidden from prying eyes. Once suitably attired, he could slip down the steps at the back of the machine into the shivery embrace of the encompassing waves. As the tide turned, all the machines had to be pulled up the beach again out of the way of the advancing flood. As one horse had several machines to move, the proprietor had to be a master of timing to ensure the last machine on the line was not left to float away on the tide.

Many horses spent the day half submerged in the salt water of the sea. By the end of the summer, they were unrecognisable from the poor creatures they had been. Many leg and feet troubles disappeared completely and the proprietor could sell one or two of his rejuvenated stock to a farmer for work on the land or even returned some to the cities to resume their former occupations.

A less salubrious fate for a poor old horse would be pulling a gipsies van. The general opinion of gipsies does not seem to have altered very much since their first appearance in Europe in the fourteenth century, when their place in the popularity stakes could not have been lower. "In the year 1417, there appeared for the first time in Germany a people uncouth, black, dirty . . . the women and children travelled in carts."

By 1893 it was estimated that there were about 12,000 gipsies in England. The 'carts' had developed into colourful vans large enough to accommodate the entire family. A gipsies van was permanent home, only means of conveyance and place of work. For a nomadic race there were few opportunities of earning a living. The men did however develop their skill as coppersmiths and workers of metal . . . The women often had a reputation for witchery. Though rarely employed in the weaving of spells, their mastery of a few charms and understanding of the rudimentary healing powers of various herbs—common to many vagrant races—was enough to give them a semblance of occult knowledge. In addition their skill in palmistry and talent for fortune telling created a sufficient aura of mystery to convince the simple minds of those with whom they came in contact.

The travelling showman lived a similarly nomadic life. In an age without cinema and television, entertainment of a far simpler kind could always attract a profitable audience. Travelling round the small villages and inaccessible country districts with a monkey or two and a performing dog, any showman with a good line in patter and a few conjuring tricks could be sure of a favourable reception. His horsedrawn cage, containing the performers for all to see, would be sufficient advertisement for him, and once he had drawn a crowd of curious spectators he could begin his act.

NONDESCRIPT

GIPSIES VAN

HAPPY FAMILY

BATHING MACHINE

Authors Note

When I began this book, I had no idea how enjoyable my search for information about William Freelove's sketches would be. The friendly and enthusiastic interest of all those whose lives are still involved with horses and carriages was most encouraging. I am particularly grateful for the hospitality and help I received from Mr. and Mrs. Sanders Watney and Mr. Walter Gilbey; as well as the happy and knowledgeable reminiscences of:—

    Mr. Bert Barley of the Knightsbridge Riding School
    Mr. Dougie Waite of Youngs Brewery
    Mr. Stanley Hilton
    Mr. Reg Brown, Secretary of the Coaching Club of Great Britain
    The staff of the Royal Mews, Buckingham Palace.

Jennifer Lang